Metal Mouth

Julie Mitchell
Heath McKenzie

Rigby

www.Rigby.com
1-800-531-5015

Rigby Focus Forward

This Edition © 2009 Rigby, a Harcourt Education Imprint

Published in 2007 by Nelson Australia Pty Ltd ACN: 058 280 149
A Cengage Learning company

All rights reserved. No part of the material protected by this copyright may be reproduced or utilized in any form or by any means, in whole or in part, without permission in writing from the copyright owner. Requests for permission should be mailed to: Paralegal Department, 6277 Sea Harbor Drive, Orlando, FL 32887.

Rigby is a trademark of Harcourt, registered in the United States of America and/or other jurisdictions.

1 2 3 4 5 6 7 8 374 14 13 12 11 10 09 08 07
Printed and bound in China

Metal Mouth
ISBN-13   978-1-4190-3738-2
ISBN-10   1-4190-3738-2

If you have received these materials as examination copies free of charge, Rigby retains title to the materials and they may not be resold. Resale of examination copies is strictly prohibited and is illegal.

Possession of this publication in print format does not entitle users to convert this publication, or any portion of it, into electronic format.

METAL Mouth

Julie Mitchell
Heath McKenzie

Contents

Chapter 1	**Bad News**	4
Chapter 2	**Stuck!**	10
Chapter 3	**A Terrible Shock**	18

Chapter 1

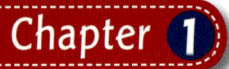

BAD NEWS

My life used to be all right.
I wasn't the best-looking kid
in my class,
but I was OK to look at.

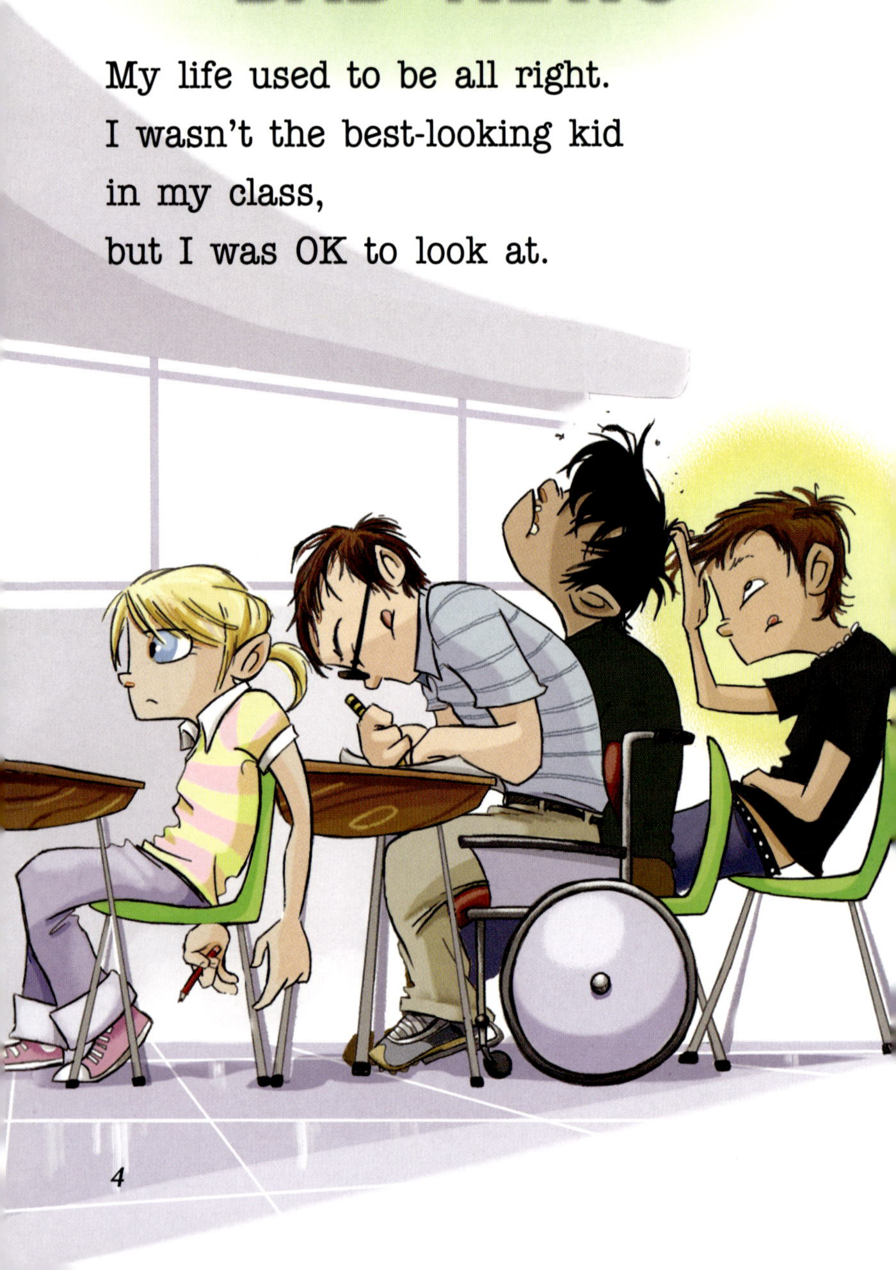

Bad News

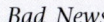

At least I didn't have braces,
like Emma Green.
She had a big old set of metal ones,
and I felt very sorry for her.

Metal Mouth

Like I said, my life was OK.
But one day I got
some very bad news.

"Brad," Mom said,
"I've just had a talk with the dentist.
She wants me to send you
to someone who can fit braces
right away."

There was more bad news.
I was getting the old kind of braces,
the same kind as Emma Green.

"No-o-o-o!!" I shouted.

Metal Mouth

A week later, I had a face full of metal.

Now there were two people in my class I felt sorry for.
One of them was me.

Chapter 2

STUCK!

Having braces was bad,
but what happened next was terrible.

One stormy afternoon,
I was walking home from school.
Suddenly there was a loud **C-R-A-C-K!**
and lightning hit the ground
in front of me.

Metal Mouth

I got a terrible scare.
I felt my hair stand up on end.

Stuck!

I told Mom about it when I got home.
But I didn't find out I had a problem
until later.

Metal Mouth

As I was putting my school notes together, something very odd happened.

Stuck!

When I ate dinner that night,
my fork stuck to my braces.

"That's not a good look, Brad,"
Mom said.
"Stop playing with your food."

"I'm not playing," I said,
pulling at the fork.
"My braces are like a magnet."

Metal Mouth

"The lightning must have done it,"
Mom said as she pulled off the fork.
"Don't worry.
I'm sure the effect won't last."

I hoped Mom was right.
The school dance was coming up,
and the girls would be wearing
lots of jewelry.
I didn't want any of it
ending up in my mouth.

Chapter 3

A TERRIBLE SHOCK

The next day,
my braces were still magnetic,
so I tried to keep my mouth shut.

But in science class, I forgot.
I said something to my friend,
and the little pieces of metal
we were using
flew up and into my mouth.

Metal Mouth

At lunchtime, I had a problem with a faucet.

A Terrible Shock

"Are you all right?"
asked a voice behind me.

I turned around.
There was Emma Green,
and she was smiling at me.

21

Metal Mouth

I opened my mouth to say,
"Yes, thanks,"
and the next thing I knew,
my braces were locked onto Emma's!

It was a terrible shock.

A Terrible Shock

But we got free.
"Sorry," I said.
"I'm having a problem with my braces."
Then I told her all about it.

She laughed.
I looked at Emma and laughed, too.

Emma and I talked for a long time.
Suddenly I understood something.

Emma and I were becoming friends, and having our braces didn't matter at all.